TI

A children's play

DAVID WOOD

SAMUEL FRENCH

LONDON
NEW YORK TORONTO SYDNEY HOLLYWOOD

TICKLE

First produced in 1972 by The Dance Drama Theatre with the following cast:

Claire Frisby
Jaki Miles
Janie Glynn
Michael O'Sullivan
Toby Sedgwick
Patrick Curtis
Leslie Portch
Gerard Bagley

Directed by Jan Colet
Designed by Susie Caulcutt
Music by David Wood

This re-written version was first produced by the Wakefield Tricycle Company at the Arts Theatre, Great Newport Street, London, on the 9th April 1977, with the following cast:

Pauline Abnar
Sharon Bower
Peter Dawson
Ian Milton
John Prior
Rob Spendlove

The Play directed by Kenneth Chubb
Settings by Jennifer Carey
Music by John Prior

CHARACTERS

The size of the cast is variable, but a minimum of six actors is required, playing several parts each. Most, if not all, of the characters can be played by either sex.

Four Sandwich-Board Men	Opera Singer
Worker	Launderette Attendant
Café Proprietor	Customer
Tickle	Fairground Barker
Traffic Warden	Acrobat
Cars, Bicycles	Mr Mighty
Businessman	Miss Balenca
Woman with Knitting	Basher Bert
Schoolchild	Little Lionel
Street Cleaner	Referee
Three Germs	Two Wrestling Seconds
Ambulance Man	Laughing Hyena
Musicians	Keeper
Conductor	

CHORUSES

WHAT AM I?	Tickle
I'M A TICKLE	Tickle
VACUUM SONG	Café Proprietor and Chorus
WHERE WILL TICKLE GO?	Chorus (and Audience)
WHERE WILL TICKLE GO? (reprise)	Tickle and Chorus (and Audience)
WAITING FOR THE BUS	Businessman, Woman with knitting, Schoolchild
SLEEPY TICKLE	Tickle
WHERE WILL TICKLE GO? (reprise)	Chorus (and Audience)
I'M A TICKLE (reprise)	Tickle
THE GERMS' SONG	The Germs
WHERE WILL TICKLE GO? (reprise)	Tickle and Chorus (and Audience)
TUMBLE TUMBLE	Chorus
THE GERMS' SONG (reprise)	The Germs
I'M A TICKLE (reprise)	Tickle
BASHER'S CHORUS	Basher
I WISH I HAD A FRIEND/ I'M A TICKLE (reprise)	Tickle
TICKLE'S FOUND A HOME/ HE'S A TICKLE	Chorus (and Audience)

PRODUCTION NOTES

The play has a minimum cast of six. Most of the characters can be played by either sex. In one production, for instance, the wrestling match was not between Basher Bert and Little Lionel, but Basher Bertha and Puny Patsy!

The play has been purposely written in a flexible manner so that the invention of ideas of cast and director may be incorporated. The action should obviously flow smoothly and be continuous. The following suggestions may be helpful.

The **songs** may be accompanied or unaccompanied. Other music may be on tape or improvised by the cast.

The **set** should be simple, perhaps incorporating rostra and poles attached to large sheets, painted or plain.

Costumes should be simple additions to basic rehearsal type clothes. It is suggested that the Germs wear masks.

Props should only be used when necessary. If they can be mimed or created imaginatively by the actor's skill and ingenuity, they should be. In a very good production by the Wakefield Tricycle Company, oversize props were very effectively made out of foam rubber.

David Wood

TICKLE

Before the play starts, four of the Actors mingle with the Audience, or, if the situation allows, rustle up their Audience by wearing sandwich-boards with slogans like "COME AND GET IT", "EGG-SELLENT FOOD", etc., on the back. Each sandwich-board has a letter—C A F and E. The Actors shout the slogans. When the Audience is assembled, the four sandwich-board bearers stand facing them—slogans to the front

An Actor, as a Worker, "enters" from the audience, talking to them, ad-libbing on the following lines

Worker Anyone seen a good place for a nosh? Time for breakfast. Where's the nearest place for a bite to eat? Etc etc.

At a given moment the boards turn round, revealing the letters. They spell "FACE"

Hey, look, there we are! Look at the sign. Café, it says. I'll try there.

The Audience should point out that it does not say "CAFE", but "FACE". The Worker pretends not to understand

Eh? Café. CAFÉ. Where you eat food! Eh? Face? What about my face? (*He realizes, turns and sees the "sign"*) Oh! FACE! You're right. (*He shouts or whistles*)

The Actors react puzzled, then realize, and shuffle themselves round to the correct spelling. They kneel down

There we are. Café. (*He "enters" the café, maybe miming a door and making the noise of a bell*)

The Proprietor "enters" and stands behind the sandwich-boards, which thus act as a counter

Morning.
Proprietor Morning, sir. What'll you have?
Worker What've you got?

Proprietor Sausages, bacon, fried bread, poached eggs, fried eggs,
    scrambled eggs, soft-boiled eggs, hard-boiled eggs, tea, coffee.
Worker Yes, please.
Proprietor What?
Worker I'll have sausages, bacon, fried bread, poached eggs,
    fried eggs, scrambled eggs, soft-boiled eggs, hard-boiled eggs,
    tea and coffee, please.
Proprietor (*to the Audience*) What a pig!
Worker (*a bit threateningly*) What?
Proprietor I said: What a—BIG—breakfast.
Worker Well, I need something to keep me going till elevenses.
Proprietor Here you are, then. (*He produces a very large plateful
    —possibly all made in one, out of polystyrene—and hands it to
    the Worker*) Sauce?
Worker Yes, please.

The Proprietor squirts on lashings of sauce

Proprietor Salt?
Worker Please.

The Proprietor shakes on salt from a huge salt-pot

Proprietor Pepper?
Worker Please.

The Proprietor shakes on pepper

    Thanks. (*He carries the plate forward, then stops, nose twitching*)
    Aaahahaha . . .
Proprietor What's the matter? (*He comes forward*)
Worker Nothing. (*Suddenly*) Tishoo!

The Proprietor is blown over by the sneeze

    Sorry. Aaahahaha.
Proprietor What is it?
Worker Nothing. Just a little tickle. In my nose. Aaaaahahaha . . .

The Proprietor warily prepares himself for the next impact

    Must be the pepper. Aaaaahaha. Just a little tickle.

The Proprietor relaxes

    Tishoo!

The Proprietor falls over again

ATISHOO!

This time, an Actor (one of the board-carriers) jumps from behind the counter, if possible looking as though he has been blown out of the Worker's nose or throat. This is Tickle. He looks wide-eyed about him. Nobody else registers his arrival

That's got rid of it. Horrible little tickle. (*He cannot hear or see Tickle. He tucks into his food*)
Proprietor I'll get your tea and coffee.
Worker Thanks.

Music or sounds as Tickle takes stock of his surroundings—almost like a newly born baby. He stands, falls, looks wide-eyed and wondering

Tickle (*singing*)
What am I?
What am I?
Where have I come from?
How did I arrive?

What am I?
What am I?
What am I doing?
Why am I alive?

What to do?
Where to go?
What am I?
I don't know.

Perhaps he starts to gain confidence, and tries to utter a word. The music or sounds reach a climax as he manages to speak

Tick—le, Tick—le. (*He notices the Audience*) Hallo. (*He raises his hand to wave and involuntarily makes a tickling movement*) Tickle. Tickle. (*He does it with his other hand*) Tick—tick— tick—tickle. I'm a tickle! (*He sings*)
I'm a Tickle,
A Tickle
A Tickle, Tickle, Tickle

I'm a Tickle
Yes I am.

I'm a Tickle,
A Tickle
A Tickle, Tickle, Tickle
I'm a Tickle
Yes I am.
   (*Throughout the song he makes his tickling movements with his hands. As he finishes, he goes up to the Worker*) I'm a Tickle.
   (*He goes up to the Proprietor*) Hey, I'm a Tickle.

They ignore him, and carry on their conversation as if he is not there

Proprietor Everything all right, then?
Worker Lovely.
Proprietor Good. I was afraid I'd spoiled it all for you with too much pepper.
Worker No, no. I just got a little tickle up my nose.
Proprietor That's all right, then. I haven't seen you in here before, have I?

Tickle, having failed to get their attention by talking to them, now tries tickling them—on their chin, leg, etc. During the following dialogue they react slightly worried, but pretend nothing is happening. Clearly they cannot see Tickle

Worker I'm new to this area. Just arrived last night. With the fair. Down on the common.
Proprietor Oh yes? I've seen the posters. Good, is it?
Worker Yes. Not bad. Pretty fair. Get it? Fair. A fair fair.

The Worker finds this very funny, but his laughter turns to a different kind when Tickle lands a particularly well-aimed tickle on him. He tries to control himself—he does not want to look silly

Proprietor Maybe I'll try and bring the kids.
Worker That would be nice.
Proprietor That's seventy-five pence, then.
Worker Right. Very reasonable, too.

As the Worker goes to hand over his money, Tickle tickles him. He drops the money, and both he and the Proprietor make a dive for

*it. Tickle starts gaily tickling them both. They fall on the floor in
hysterics, rolling about on each other. Finally, embarrassed, they
get up. The Worker hands the Proprietor the money*

I'll—er—be seeing you, then.

*As the Worker walks out, Tickle tickles him. He giggles. The
Proprietor gives him an odd look*

The Worker goes

Proprietor Yes. (*He begins to clear away*) You don't half get some
funny people in here.

Tickle tickles the Proprietor

The Proprietor suddenly laughs very loudly, and hurries off

Tickle Hey, come back! Come back! Please. (*He gives up, and
walks towards the Audience*) She can't hear me. I don't think
she can see me, either. I don't understand it. *You* can hear me,
can't you? Can you see me, too?

The Proprietor enters to clear away more crockery, etc.

Tickle sees her and chases after her again, calling

Hey, come back! I'm a Tickle . . .

The Proprietor goes

*Tickle is stopped in his tracks by a strange sound—possibly made
by the other Actors. It is the noise of a vacuum-cleaner*

*The Proprietor enters with a huge prop vacuum-cleaner—this
could be an Actor inside a giant bag with an over-size tube and
sucking attachment*

*Tickle retreats, terrified. The humming and sucking noises continue,
as an accompaniment*

Proprietor (*singing or speaking*)
    Suck, suck, suck
    Goes the vac—u—um;
    Suck, suck, suck,
    Suck up ev'ry crumb . . .

This is repeated as necessary. Tickle does not realize what is going on. He is pulled unwillingly towards the vacuum-cleaner, and struggles to get away. Eventually he is "caught", and clogs the machine; the noises judder to a stop

I don't know what's the matter with this machine—always getting its works clogged up.

The Proprietor manages to shake Tickle off, but then gets caught up herself. The humour of this could be extended to include the machine "getting out of control", and trying to suck up members of the Audience. Tickle hides in fright

Eventually the Proprietor exits, singing another chorus of "Suck, suck, suck"

Tickle emerges nervously

Tickle Has it gone?

Audience participation

What kind of a person was that?
Not a person? Well, what was it, then?
What's a vacuum-cleaner?
I'm not dirty. Why was it after me?
Tell you what; I'm getting out of here. With that noisy machine around, it's not safe.

Tickle escapes, and goes off. The rest of the Cast come together and sing

All Where will Tickle go?
Where will Tickle roam?
Tickle's in a pickle, for he hasn't a home.
An Actor (*to the Audience*) Hey, I've got an idea. This song crops up again in the story, doesn't it?

The others confirm this

Then why doesn't everyone—(*taking in the Audience*)—join in? Help us out a bit. Would you like to do that? All right. Let's have a practice.

The Actor leads the Audience in learning the song. They all sing it a couple of times, then do it "for real"

As the song is sung, the Actors melt away, and Tickle enters

Tickle That's better. Free at last.

A Traffic Warden enters and moves C, *possibly standing on a podium*

(*Noticing the Traffic Warden and whispering*) What's that?
Audience A traffic warden.
Tickle Really? What's a traffic warden? Do you think he/she might know somewhere safe where I can hide from noisy machines? All right, I'll ask.

Tickle starts moving towards the Traffic Warden, but sudden noises of traffic make him jump and look round

Actors now become cars, bicycles, etc., coming from both directions, hooting, ringing bells

The Traffic Warden directs the traffic with exaggerated arm signals. Tickle tries to get through the traffic to speak to the Traffic Warden but has difficulty doing so. He has to jump madly out of the way. Finally, he succeeds. There is a lull in the traffic

Tickle, tickle. Excuse me.

Tickle involuntarily tickles the Traffic Warden, making him/her jump, giggle, and momentarily drop his/her arms

Sorry. Tickle, tickle.

The traffic starts to enter again. Tickle tickles the Traffic Warden again, with the same reaction. The arms drop, and the traffic is uncertain what to do. Recovering, the Traffic Warden beckons one lot of traffic to proceed

Can you help me, please? Tickle, tickle. (*He gives a bigger tickle*)

The tickle works even more strongly. The arms drop, and the Traffic Warden is confused. He/she starts again and beckons the other lot of traffic, without stopping the first. He/she is laughing because of the tickle and his/her arms flail uncontrollably. Cars crash into one another, and those behind concertina into them. Chaos—horns hooting, etc. Tickle looks mystified

First Driver (*to the Traffic Warden*) What on earth do you think you're doing?

Second Driver Stop laughing. Look at my beautiful car.
Traffic Warden Ha, ha, ha. Something tickled me. Ha, ha.
First Driver Tickled you?
Second Driver You'll laugh on the other side of your face in a
  minute.
Traffic Warden Ha, ha, ha.

*A fight breaks out. Tickle is caught in the middle and receives many
of the blows*

Tickle (*trying to attract the attention of the Driver, who of course
  cannot see him*) It was my fault. I'm sorry. I tickled him/her.
  I only wanted somewhere safe to go. I didn't mean—listen,
  please . . . (*Extricating himself, he limps away*)

The Traffic Warden and the Drivers exit, arguing furiously

(*Singing*)
  No-one seems to like a tickle
  I keep ending up in the way
  I don't want to be a nuisance, but
  I just want a place to stay.

*From now on the Audience is encouraged to join in the chorus every
time it is sung*

All Where will Tickle go?
  Where will Tickle roam?
  Tickle's in a pickle, for he hasn't a home.
Tickle I don't understand it. All of those noisy machines charg-
  ing around trying to squash me flat. And that—what did you
  call him/her?—traffic warden—he/she didn't even try to help.
  Didn't even *notice* me. (*Pause*) Nobody notices me. Oh dear.
  Does that mean they couldn't see me either? Like in the café.
  How can I get anyone to help me find somewhere safe to go if
  they can't see me? (*Pause*) I know. If I try to act just like people
  do, perhaps they'll think I'm one of them, and be able to see me!
  Let's see. I'll act just like—him!

*A Businessman enters, pompously walking along in a deter-
mined manner. He wears a bowler and spectacles, and carries a
newspaper*

Tickle follows him, and imitates his every movement

A Bus Stop enters, accompanied by a Woman knitting, and a Schoolchild eating an ice-cream. They are in the bus queue

The Businessman joins the bus queue, and Tickle tags on the end, copying every movement—e.g. opening a newspaper, looking impatiently at his wristwatch, etc. The three at the bus stop sing, and Tickle makes an attempt to join in

Businessman
Woman
Schoolchild *(singing)*

We're waiting for the bus
Waiting for the bus
We've been waiting half the afternoon
We're waiting for the bus
Waiting for the bus
Hurry up and get here soon.

Tickle, unable to resist, tickles the Businessman

Tickle Tickle, tickle!

The Businessman reacts by jumping, not laughing, then he drops his paper. As he picks it up he drops his glasses, then his hat. As he picks up one thing, the other drops, etc. When he is back to normal, Tickle tickles him again. He reacts, thinks, looks slowly towards the Woman next to him, and furiously accuses her.

Businessman How dare you, madam!
Woman What?
Businessman Kindly keep your hands to yourself.
Woman Excuse me, I . . .
Businessman It's extremely rude to tickle a perfect stranger.
Woman I . . . Oooh!
Tickle Tickle, tickle!

The Woman stops, as Tickle now tickles her. She reacts and looks shocked. Tickle does it again. She turns to the Businessman

Woman What a cheek!
Businessman I beg your pardon?
Woman First you accuse me of tickling you, then you tickle *me*. Ooh!

The Woman is tickled again, but as she is looking at the Businessman, it cannot have been by him

Oh, I've dropped a stitch. (*She bends down to look for it*)

Businessman I hope you're satisfied.
Woman How do you mean?
Businessman That I didn't tickle you.
Woman Then who was it?

They both turn and look at the Schoolchild eating ice cream

Businessman
Woman }It was you! (*Speaking together*)
Schoolchild What?

Businessman
Woman }You—tickler, you. (*Speaking together*)
Schoolchild What?

Businessman
Woman }You tickled me. (*Speaking together*)
Schoolchild Didn't.

Businessman
Woman }Did. (*Speaking together*)
Schoolchild Didn't.

Businessman
Woman }Did. (*Speaking together*)
Tickle Tickle, tickle.

Tickle tickles the child, who reacts with a violent jump, smashing the ice-cream into the Woman's face. All three argue with one another. Tickle finds this very amusing

   The Bus enters, possibly a painted sheet carried by two Actors. It stops

The arguing trio do not see the Bus. Tickle sees it and realizes that, thanks to him, they are arguing so much they will miss it. He tries to attract their attention

   Hey, look—the bus! Hey! Quick. You'll miss it. (*To the Audience*) It's no good. They can't hear me!

   The Bus goes "ding ding" and exits. The arguing trio see it, and react, shouting, as they dash after it, trying to get it to stop. The Businessman drops his newspaper as he runs off

Tickle shrugs his shoulders and sits "in the gutter". He yawns a huge yawn

   (*To the Audience*) What was that? A yawn? Why did I do

that? Because I'm what? Tired? What's the best thing to do if I'm tired? Go to sleep? How do I do that? Lie down and close my eyes? Oh, all right, though it seems a stupid thing to do. Is it safe? (*He starts to lie down*) It's a bit cold. How could I keep warm?

This section is improvized, and Audience reaction encouraged. If desired, Tickle can develop this conversation by asking questions about "Home", "Bed", "Sheets", "Shelter", "Security", etc., all the things Tickle lacks. The Audience may suggest that Tickle uses the Businessman's dropped newspaper as sheets. Eventually he settles for the night

(*Singing*)
    I'm a sleepy Tickle
    With nowhere to go
    I'm a sleepy Tickle
    But I haven't got a home
    No-one to look after me
    Nowhere safe to stay
    No warm bed to snuggle in—
    I just wander round all day . . .
(*He yawns and stretches*)

The other Actors sing with the Audience, a slow, tired version of the chorus

All   (*singing*)
    Where will Tickle go?
    Where will Tickle roam?
    Tickle's in a pickle, for he hasn't a home.

By the end of the chorus, Tickle is asleep

  A Street-cleaner enters with a large brush, whistling. He sees the newspaper. He approaches, sweeping hard

Tickle is swept along with the newspaper

  A Rubbish Tip enters—perhaps made of a coloured sheet, with Actors under it to make it move, ripple, etc. These Actors are the Germs who emerge later in the scene. (Alternatively a large dustbin may be used)

The Street-cleaner carefully picks up the newspaper and throws it into the tip/bin. As he turns away the paper flies out again, surprising him. He throws it in again. Again it flies back. He starts to throw it in, but thinks better of it. Suddenly a siren sounds (or an alarm clock goes off, which the Street-cleaner takes from his pocket and bangs until it stops ringing). It is one o'clock—lunchtime. The Street-cleaner knocks off work and takes out an oversize prop sandwich, and an oversize drink can complete with fixed straw. He takes a drink, keeping his sandwich on his other, outstretched hand. He starts reading a page of the newspaper. Suddenly, accompanied by sinister sounds if possible, a strange, evil character emerges from the rubbish—he is a Germ. He sees the sandwich, creeps up to it, checks that nobody is looking, and lifts the top of the sandwich and breathes or spits on it. The Audience may shout out a warning to the Street-cleaner, but he takes no notice. The Germ finishes the dastardly deed, then returns to the rubbish. The Street-cleaner finishes his drink and throws the can away. Perhaps he throws it into the rubbish, in which case the Germ shouts "Ow!", and the Street-cleaner reacts bemused. He bites greedily into his sandwich, chews a bit, then carefully replaces the rest inside his coat. He starts work again, returns to where Tickle is still asleep, and tries again to sweep him up

Tickle (*waking*) Whoa! Stop it! Get off! Etc.

Suddenly the Street-cleaner starts having paroxysms as the Germ's deed does it worst. He writhes and jerks around, clutching his stomach. Tickle watches, fascinated and a little frightened

> *An ambulance siren loudly heralds the arrival of the Ambulance: one Actor with a cut-out*

In a "silent-film"-type sequence, the Ambulance Man leaves his vehicle and goes to help the gasping Street-cleaner. He bandages his patient with great speed—a bandage being a sovereign remedy— until the Street-cleaner cannot move. Tickle watches, and asks the Audience questions

> What's that long white stuff? Bandage? What's that for? Why does *he* need a bandage? He doesn't look very happy.

From the above, Tickle gleans the information that the Street-cleaner is ill and is being rushed to hospital. The Ambulance Man returns to his vehicle, whistles, and beckons the Street-cleaner to hop on board: but the Street-cleaner shakes his head—he cannot move. He tries hobbling towards the ambulance. Tickle sees what is going on

Shall I help?

Tickle approaches the Street-cleaner kindly, but every time he touches him—to help him along—he tickles the poor man, who finds it very painful to laugh while bandaged. Tickle is not trying to tickle; he just automatically tickles by touching. Eventually, the Street-cleaner struggles aboard the Ambulance

The Ambulance streaks off, siren wailing

Tickle is left alone

I hope he's all right. I wonder why he got ill. (*He gets nearer the tip/bin—and reacts to the smell*) Pooh! What a pong.

Unseen by Tickle, the Germ emerges from the rubbish. The Audience shouts a warning

What? Where?

Tickle turns, but the Germ has disappeared

I can't see anything. There's nothing there!

The Germ appears again. Audience reaction, pantomime-style

I don't want to go and look. It smells awful. Oh, all right . . .

The Germ disappears as Tickle turns to look

Hey! You're having me on, aren't you? There's nothing there at all.

Suddenly we all hear murmurings and mumblings from inside the tip/bin

There *is* something there. (*He begins to back away*)

The Mumps Germ emerges slowly and menacingly over the tip. Mumps takes a good look at Tickle, disappears, then emerges again with another Germ—Laryngitis. Both look at Tickle, then at each other, then disappear. They emerge again with the Head Germ—Big G. Tickle is really frightened, but tries a tentative wave

Who are you?

Mumps indicates to Laryngitis (Larry) to go down to Tickle

Larry Who are *you*?
Tickle Who? Me?

Larry nods

They can see me!
Larry Who are you?
Tickle Tickle. (*He sings*)
I'm a Tickle
A Tickle
A Tickle, Tickle, Tickle
I'm a Tickle
Yes I am.

I'm a Tickle
A Tickle
A Tickle, Tickle, Tickle
I'm a Tickle
Yes I am.

During the above, Larry and Mumps pick up the rhythm of the music and begin to dance. They carry on even when the music stops. Tickle enjoys this

Big G (*interrupting their dance*) What's a tickle?

In the following sequence, all questions are passed down the line of Germs. Big G asks the questions in a loud and unintelligible mumble. Mumps repeats the question in a not quite distinguishable way, and Laryngitis says it finally clearly so Tickle can understand

Tickle Well—don't you know what a tickle is? Oh. Well, when I do it to people, it makes them shake and wobble and jump.

No response

Look, I'll show you. You tickle them, like this. (*He makes the tickling motion in the air*)

Larry looks uncertain, but makes a similar motion

Under their arms or on their noses.

Larry goes and tickles Mumps' nose. No response. Mumps tickles Big G. No response

Well, it usually works. I'll do it to you. (*He tickles Larry's nose*)

Larry laughs loudly and scratches his nose

Larry Ohhhh!

Larry goes and tickles Mumps again. No response. Mumps turns to Big G. Big shrug

Tickle Well, I suppose I'll have to tickle all of you.

Tickle approaches Mumps and tickles his neck. Mumps laughs—a big deep laugh. Tickle laughs, too. Suddenly he is driven off as Big G, very aggressively, marches on him, pointing to his nose. Tickle very gingerly tickles him. An enormous laugh from Big G makes Tickle relax. Again Big G approaches aggressively and demands a tickle. This time Tickle tickles the top of his head: another huge laugh. Then, suddenly, Big G's mood changes to one of aggressive seriousness

Big G (*passing down the line*) What does he want?
Tickle I want somewhere to stay. Somewhere safe, with no nasty noisy machines.
Big G (*passing down the line*) He can stay here if he helps us.
Tickle Here? In this smelly old rubbish tip?

The Germs react very surprised. They breathe deeply, enjoyably

Germs It's not smelly. It's—nice!
Tickle Oh—well, all right. I'll stay. At least you can see me. But —who are you?
Germs (*passing up the line—Larry, Mumps, Big G.*) Who are we?

Big G gives a long, unintelligible mumble

Tickle I'm sorry, I didn't quite catch all that.

Mumps whispers to Larry

Larry Germs.
Tickle Derms?
Larry No. Germs.
Tickle Germs. But what do you do?
Germs (*passing up the line*) What do we do? What do we do? Do? Do? Do?

*The Germs come forward, menacingly singing, ending up near
Tickle*

Germs (*singing*)
> We're the Germs
> The Germs
> Who carry disease
> Then spread it around
> Making you cough and sneeze and wheeze
> We're the Germs
> The Germs
> Who give you temperatures and spots
> And Tickle can help us—ha, ha, ha, ha—LOTS!

*Tickle enjoys the song, beating time to it, not understanding the im-
plications*

Tickle But what do you *do*?
Larry Infect.
Tickle Infect? That sounds like fun.
Big G Tenshun!

*The Germs stand to attention in line, Tickle at the end, waiting for
their jobs. Big G mumbles to Mumps*

> *Mumps salutes, repeats the instruction "Fairground", and
> marches off*

Tickle Where's he going?
Larry The fairground.
Tickle Fairground?

*Big G mumbles about sending Larry to the Albert Hall to infect the
Opera Singer. Larry nods his understanding. Larry and Tickle
salute*

> *Big G shakes Tickle's hand, then laughs heartily and exits*

Tickle Where are we going?
Larry Albert Hall.
Tickle Albert who?
Larry Albert Hall.
Tickle Oh.
Larry Come on, then.

Larry and Tickle exit, then immediately reappear, as if it is the Albert Hall

Tickle Ooooh. Isn't it a big place. (*He calls*) Hellooooo!

An echo replies from back stage

Echo (*off*) Hellooooo!
Tickle I'm a Tiiickle!
Echo (*off*) You're a Tickle.

Members of the Orchestra start entering on the other side of the stage

Tickle (*noticing them*) Hey, Larry. Who are they?
Larry The Orchestra.
Tickle Orchestra? What do they do?
Larry Play.

The Orchestra begins to tune up. Tickle watches, fascinated, and mimics them. The Orchestra stops

Ssssh!

The Conductor enters

The Orchestra applauds. The Conductor comes c, bows, then turns and indicates the Opera Singer

The Opera Singer enters, to much applause

The Conductor leads her on, presents her, and returns to his place. The music begins. The Opera Singer begins to sing an operatic song, e.g. "O for the Wings of a Dove"

Tickle What a lovely noise! And look how wide she opens her mouth!
Larry You go and jump inside.
Tickle Inside what?
Larry Her mouth, stupid. And given her throat a good tickle.
Tickle Why?
Larry Stop asking questions. You do your job and then, when she's all unsuspecting, I'll do mine. (*He cackles*) Go on.

Tickle hesitates, but is pushed forward. He jumps into the Opera Singer's mouth—either using mime, or a prop head for the Singer

Tickle Tickle, tickle!

The Opera Singer suddenly coughs and the song grinds to an undignified halt. The Conductor looks annoyed. He starts the musicians again. The lady starts to sing

Tickle, tickle! (*He tickles her again*)

She coughs again, more violently. The music stops again

Conductor What is-a the matter?

Singer I'm-a sorry. I have a leetle teeckle in-a my throat. Can-a we start-a again? (*She clears her throat*)

The song starts again. Perhaps we see Tickle's hand tickling her throat. She coughs—very violently

Conductor What is-a the matter *now*?

Singer I'm-a so sorry. I still have a leetle teeckle. Could I please-a have-a my throat spray?

Conductor Throat spray.

The Conductor brings her a large throat spray. She opens her mouth. He sprays with force. As he returns, Tickle screams and "emerges" —very wet. The Conductor drops the spray on the ground

Singer Mi, mi, mi, mi. You, you, you, you. That's-a better. The-a teeckle is-a gone.

Tickle The-a teeckle is-a soaking-a wet!

The Singer prepares to sing again

Larry Right, you've done your bit. Out of my way, Tickle. My turn.

Tickle What are you going to do?

Larry Laryngitis by name, laryngitis by nature. After the tickle in the throat, the *sore* throat—(*his voice rising*)—she loses her voice and can't sing any more. (*He cackles and goes towards the mouth*)

Tickle But I like her singing. I won't let you.

Larry Out of the way. (*He knocks Tickle to one side and crawls in the Singer's mouth*)

After a moment, the Singer grinds to a halt

Conductor (*very irately, jumping up and down*) What's-a the matter *now*?

The Singer mumbles in a squeaky voice

You've lost-a your voice?

The Singer squeaks

You've got laryngitis! You're ruined.

The Singer begins to cry. Larry "emerges" from her mouth

The Conductor leads the Opera Singer off

(*As he goes*) I'm-a sorry, ladies and gentlemen, the concert is-a cancelled. Very sorry. (*To the Singer*) You'll-a never work again, you know. It's-a back to Rome for you.

The Orchestra shrugs and leaves

Tickle (*running after the Singer*) Don't go. Please don't go. I like your singing. Don't go. (*He meets Larry*)

Larry She can't sing any more, stupid. We've seen to that.

Tickle *You've* seen to it. Not me. I liked her singing.

Larry Rubbish!

Tickle I liked her singing. Ever since I was born awful things have kept happening to me. Noise and confusion and nowhere to go, and the first nice thing that happens, you go and ruin it.

Larry It's our job.

Tickle It's not mine.

Larry It is now.

Tickle But I don't want to ruin things.

Larry Goody-goody.

Tickle I don't want to live with you, anyway. Your home smells.

Larry You haven't got any choice—now. (*He approaches Tickle menacingly*) Big G will have to deal with you.

Tickle No! (*He picks up the throat spray which the Singer has left behind and sprays Larry*)

Larry screams and begins to wilt. He starts to exit

Larry (*as he goes*) You'll pay for this, Tickle. You wait. We'll get you for this.

Larry exits

Tickle I've really done it now. I've got nowhere to hide, and those Germs will be after me, and that big one—oooh! (*He sings*)

> Got to get away and quickly
> Down the road and up the hill;
> I don't want to help those Germs out, no
> I don't want to make people ill.
> (*He starts walking on the spot*)

All (*including the Audience, speeding up the chorus as Tickle runs*)
> Where will Tickle go?
> Where will Tickle roam?
> Tickle's in a pickle, for he hasn't a home.

Tickle And I'm a soaking wet Tickle, too. Give us a shout if you see anywhere I can get dry, will you? Thanks. (*He walks along the "road", still walking on the spot*)

> *Actors pass behind Tickle carrying shop signs such as "Greengrocer", "Ironmonger", "Supermarket", etc. Eventually one marked "Launderette" appears*

The Audience should shout out that here is the place to go

> Where? (*Mispronouncing it*) Lawnderetty?

The Audience correct him

> Launderette. Oh, thanks. Let's have a look. (*He "enters" the "Launderette"*) Now where?

The Actor turns round the "Launderette" sign. On the other side it reads "Spin Dryer"

> *Other Actors enter with the machine, or assemble as the machine. Whichever staging is used, it is necessary to have a dial showing varying degrees of heat*

> What does that say?

The Audience tell him

> That sounds just the job. (*He jumps in*)

> *A Launderette Attendant and a Customer enter, staggering under the weight of a basket of washing*

Attendant This way, dearie.
Customer Heavy work, the weekly wash, eh?
Attendant Yes, won't be so heavy when it's dry, dearie.

*They throw the washing into the machine, hitting Tickle, who reacts.
They close the door*

   Right. Turn the dial. Press the button. There she goes.

*The Actors blow to suggest the hot air. Then the "machine" begins
to turn. The "machine" makes noises and begins to tumble Tickle
and the washing round and round and up and down. It starts slowly
and gradually increases its speed*

Chorus
       Tumble, tumble
       Round and round
       Over and over
       Up off the ground
       Tumble, tumble
       Fly, fly, fly
       Spin, spin, spin
       Until you're dry.

The verse is repeated as desired, possibly speeding up each time

Attendant All done, dearie.
Customer Ta.

They open the door. Tickle throws out some of the clothes

   What's all this, then?
Attendant What, dearie?
Customer The dryer's throwing my clothes all over the floor.
Attendant I'll get the man to look at it when he comes around
   next week.
Customer Next week! What about today? Just look at my wash.
   It's filthy.
Attendant Maybe you should use Bold.
Customer It's not my soap, it's your machine—throwing things
   all over the place. What'll Henry say when he sees this?
Attendant Here. Look. (*He picks up a piece*) It'll brush off.
   (*Brushing the washing with her hand*) See? It's fine. Anyway,
   I'll give you a free spin next time you come in.
Customer Well—all right. (*Pause*) Are you going to the Bingo
   tonight?
Attendant Not tonight. I said I'd take the kids to the fair.

Customer Fair? Where?
Attendant Down on the common.
Customer See you, then. Have a nice time.
Attendant Ta. Tata.

The Attendant and Customer exit, chatting

Tickle, who has by now recuperated from his spin, comes out of the machine and tickles the Customer as she goes out of the door. The Customer giggles. Tickle sits down beside the dryer

Tickle Well, at least I'm dry. And it's warm here. Maybe I'll just stay for a while.

We hear the Germs singing, off

Germs (*singing*)
>   We're the Germs
>   The Germs
>   Who carry disease
>   Then spread it around
>   Making you cough and sneeze and wheeze
>   We're the Germs
>   The Germs
>   Who give you temperatures and spots
>   And Tickle's in trouble—ha, ha, ha, ha—LOTS!

During the song, Mumps and Larry enter with a net

Tickle backs away from them around the dryer

Big G enters

Tickle suddenly bumps into him. As the song ends, they throw a net over Tickle's head, and formally commence a "trial"

Big G (*in a mumble*) You were supposed to help us.
Mumps (*passing down to Larry*) You were supposed to help us.
Larry (*to Tickle*) You were supposed to help us and you didn't.
Tickle But I didn't know you were going to hurt people.
Larry It's my job. Infect.
Tickle But that singer—she didn't do anything to hurt you. What did she do to hurt you? She had a lovely voice.
Germs (*conferring together, mimicking Tickle mockingly*) What did she do to hurt you? She had a lovely voice—etc., etc.

Tickle gets up and begins to tiptoe away, but the Germs see and begin a chase. Tickle, perhaps at the Audience's suggestion or on his own, finally realizes that all he can do is tickle them—so he begins, and manages to tickle Larry and Big G into the dryer

> *Mumps, seeing what is happening, throws the net over his head and escapes*

Tickle bangs shut the dryer door and then sees the temperature gauge. He turns on the machine

Tickle (*to the Audience*) Shall I? Hotter? White Hot? Phew!

The Germs scream and disintegrate in the machine

> That's got rid of them, then. No? Who got away? Mumps? Oh no. Where did he go? Where? That's right. Big G told Mumps to work at the fairground today—to infect all the people. (*He sings*)
>
> Got to get a move on quickly
> Got to catch up with Mumps
> Before he infects all the people
> Before he gives them lumps and bumps.
>
> I'm a Tickle
> A Tickle
> A Tickle, Tickle, Tickle
> I'm a Tickle
> Yes I am.

Tickle runs off. A Fairground Barker enters to circus music. He is juggling or displaying some other entertaining skill

Barker Follow me. Follow me. This way, ladies and gentlemen, boys and girls. Billy Joy's tremendous travelling fair. For three nights only—all the fun of the fair. Down on your local common. See Mr Mighty—the strongest man in the world; Miss Balenca, and her agile acrobatics. And in the wrestling-ring we present Basher Bert from Bermondsey meeting Little Lionel from Leytonstone; and all the way from Africa, at tremendous expense, the fabulous laughing hyena. Come one, come all. To Billy Joy's travelling fair.

Tickle enters during the above speech. He now follows the Barker off

Tickle If he's going to the fair, I'll follow him.

Music comes up again

 *The Barker and Tickle enter from the opposite side. The Barker is
still juggling. The Fairground "appears"*

*Whatever skills in this area each Actor possesses should be used.
There is, say, an Acrobat doing cartwheels and headstands, and Mr
Mighty preparing for the big lift. Tickle takes one of the balls out
of the Juggler's hand, then tickles the Acrobat, ruining her act. He
takes another ball out of the Juggler's hand. The Juggler is very confused. Tickle throws the balls back to him. Mr Mighty begins his
big lift. Tickle watches. When the weights are above his head, Tickle
pushes up, first on one side and then on the other side, to confuse Mr
Mighty, then tickles him. Mr Mighty collapses in laughter, swinging
the featherweight weights in one hand. When he realizes he has been
exposed as a fake, he tries to hide the weight behind his back and
slink off*

Barker Thank you, Mr Mighty. And now, on the tightrope, Miss
 Balenca.

 *Mr Mighty exits. Music. Miss Balenca enters, curtsies, and
begins (in mime) her walk along the tightrope*

*Tickle watches her, then jumps on the rope. Miss Balenca begins to
lose her balance and just manages to make it to safety. She looks
confused, but presents herself to the Audience again, and as the
music starts she begins to walk. Tickle once again interrupts the
act by awkwardly walking along the rope as well. He pushes the
rope down, she springs up; as Tickle comes up, she is forced down,
etc. Finally he tickles her and she falls off in great confusion.*

The Barker hurriedly intervenes

 Get off with you, get off!

 Miss Balenca goes off

During the following a "ring" is set up, with stools and seconds

 Very sorry, ladies and gentlemen. (*He rings a bell*) And now
 we present all-star wrestling. The fight of the century: between
 —in the blue corner, that renowned pugilist—Basher Bert from
 Bermondsey!

Basher enters—huge muscles, very aggressive and tough. He stills the cheers

Basher I float like a butterfly
I sting like a bee
And I'll pulverize Lionel—
Wait and see! Yeh.

Barker (*as Referee*) All right, Basher. And his opponent. His first time in the ring—in the red corner, Little Lionel from Leytonstone!

Lionel enters. He is tiny—in trousers much too big for him

The Barker, as Referee, checks their nails and feet

Come here. I want a good clean fight. No kicking or biting or putting your tongues out. Now, shake hands.

Bert takes Lionel's hand and squeezes so hard that Lionel is forced to his knees

Seconds away. Round One.

The bell sounds. The wrestling starts with the Referee (Barker) controlling the wrestlers. The mime should be funny. Basher Bert is seen to be much the stronger. Little Lionel does not stand a chance. As soon as he gets up he is knocked down again. The wrestlers find themselves in odd convoluted knotted positions, and get muddled as to whose leg is whose, etc. Maybe Basher Bert bites Lionel. At any rate, the battle is accompanied by all the grunts and groans and tortured faces which are so familiar and amusing in television wrestling. During this first round, Tickle points out any unfair play by Basher Bert. Eventually Basher Bert is seen to gain a "fall". Boos are heard

Ladies and gentlemen, in the first round, a double reverse backward leghold hammer-throw pinfall to Basher Bert. And here is the action replay.

The wrestlers perform the closing seconds of the round in slow motion, the Referee (Barker) and crowd obviously joining in. As the replay ends, the wrestlers return to their corners. Tickle comes forward

Tickle (*to the Audience*) Who do you want to win? Yes, I want Little Lionel to win, too. I wonder if I could help.

Barker (*as Referee*) Round Two.

Lionel is weakening fast. After a short while there is an incident during which the Referee (Barker) gets hit my mistake. Lionel looks certain of defeat. Tickle watches, affected by the injustice of the fight. He jumps into the ring, stalks Bert, chooses his moment and, at a crucial stage, tickles him unmercifully until he is reduced to a hysterical jelly. Lionel has only to swing him into a corner post a couple of times and Bert is out for the count

(*Probably joined by the Audience*) One, two, three, four, five, six, seven, eight, nine, OUT!

Basher (*dazed*) It's not fair. I was tickled. Wasn't I tickled? Etc.

Basher Bert is led away and exits. Little Lionel, the Barker and the wrestling ring go, too

Tickle Hey, I did it. I did it, didn't I? I helped somebody instead of making things go wrong. I feel really good about that. But Little Lionel didn't *know* I'd helped him. That's the trouble. Nobody can see me. Except those Germs. And they're no good.

(*He sings*)
    I wish I had a friend
    Who could see me
    I wish I had a friend
    Who could hear what I say
    Someone to care for
    Someone to share with
    If only I could find a friend today
    But I won't
    Because

    I'm a Tickle
    A Tickle
    A Tickle, Tickle, Tickle
    I'm a Tickle
    Yes, I am.

Tickle exits, sadly. The Laughing Hyena enters with his Keeper. The Hyena looks very miserable

Keeper Come on, Herman. You're supposed to be a laughing Hyena, not a crying one. I traded two chimps and a liberty horse for you, mate, and if you don't laugh I'll lose my job. We've got to go on in a minute. Now laugh, Herman. You've got to laugh.

Nothing but sad groans from the Hyena

I don't understand it. I've been cheated.

The Keeper, exasperated, exits. Tickle enters, and sees the Hyena

Tickle What's that?

The Audience tell him

But he's not laughing. What's the matter with him?

The Hyena makes a pleading noise

He doesn't look too good.

The Hyena looks right at Tickle, and groans

Can you see me?

The Hyena nods

He can see me. Can you hear me?
Hyena Of course I can.
Tickle He can hear me, too. But why are you looking so sad?
Hyena I don't feel well.
Tickle It's Mumps. It's Mumps, isn't it? He's infected you. Where is that nasty Germ? (*He begins to hunt for Mumps*)

As Tickle goes in one direction, Mumps enters surreptitiously in the other

The Audience shout out Mumps' whereabouts, but, in pantomime fashion, Tickle keeps missing him; Mumps manages to hide in time whenever Tickle turns

Where? Over there? Where? Etc. (*Finally he spots him*) So it *is* you, Mumps. Well, you're not going to get away with it this time. Laugh, Mr Hyena, laugh. I'll make you feel better.

Tickle tickles the Hyena, who feebly tries to laugh. Mumps waits a minute, then breathes his terrible germs over the Hyena, who groans and collapses

Laugh, please laugh.

The Hyena laughs, but immediately Mumps breathes on him again and he groans and collapses

This doesn't seem to be working.

The Keeper enters. He cannot see Tickle

Keeper Here you are, Herman. I've got some medicine for you. You take it, and maybe you'll be able to laugh.

The Hyena turns away

Don't play games with me, you stupid animal. Take your medicine.

Tickle Take it, Herman. Maybe it'll get rid of the Germ. Then you'll feel better and we can have fun together. (*Pause*) You can be my friend.

Keeper I'm warning you, Herman.

Tickle Go on, take it.

The Hyena takes the medicine

Keeper That's better. Don't know what's got into you, I really don't.

The Keeper exits

At the same moment as the Hyena reacts to the medicine by turning healthy, accompanied by sound effects, Mumps begins to writhe around in a death agony. He sinks to the floor and dies. Tickle cheers. The Hyena begins to laugh, small laughs at first, but getting more and more raucous

Hyena Oh, thank you, thank you—what's your name?

Tickle Tickle.

Hyena Thank you, Tickle.

Tickle It was nothing.

Hyena Tickle. Could you stay with me, do you think? I'm afraid of him, you know—that man. He's awfully bad-tempered and he gets very angry when I don't laugh. You could live here with me and we could do things together and be friends.

Tickle I'd like that.

   The Keeper enters

Keeper What's the matter now, then? Talking to yourself?
Tickle Cheer up, Mr Keeper.

He tickles the Keeper, who roars with laughter. The Hyena laughs at him

Keeper You're laughing. You're happy. I'm happy. Everybody's happy.

   The whole cast enters

All (*singing*)
     Tickle's gonna be all right now—
     He's happy as he can be;
     He's got a home, got a friend now,
     As you can clearly see—

     Tickle's found a home
     Tickle's found a home
     He's not in a pickle, now he's found a new home.
An Actor (*shouting*) Come on, everybody join in!
All (*including the Audience*)
     Tickle's found a home
     Tickle's found a home
     He's not in a pickle, now he's found a new home.
Tickle Who wants a tickle, then?

During the following chorus Tickle moves into the Audience, tickling children, getting them to tickle one another, etc.

All (*singing*)
     He's a Tickle
     A Tickle
     A Tickle, Tickle, Tickle
     And now it's
     Time to say

Tickle returns to the rest of the cast

All (*singing*)
     And we're happy

We're happy
We're happy, happy, happy
That we met you all today.

Everyone waves and says "Good-bye", as—

the CURTAIN *falls*

FURNITURE AND PROPERTY LIST

Properties mentioned in the text are listed below, but see the Author's Note on p. vi

On stage: Bare rostra, poles attached to painted or plain sheets

Off stage: 4 sandwich boards lettered C.A.F.E. on reverse **(Sandwich-Board Bearers)**
Large plateful of "eggs", etc. **(Proprietor)**
Sauce bottle, salt and pepper pots **(Proprietor)**
Money **(Worker)**
Vacuum cleaner **(Proprietor)**
Newspaper, bowler hat, spectacles, watch **(Businessman)**
Ice cream **(Schoolchild)**
Knitting **(Bus Woman)**
"Bus" **(Actors)**
Brush **(Street-Cleaner)**
"Rubbish tip" **(Germs)**
Alarm clock **(Street-Cleaner)**
Oversize prop sandwich, drink can, straw **(Street-Cleaner)**
"Ambulance" **(Actor)**
Bandage **(Ambulance Man)**
"Musical instruments" **(Orchestra)**
Large throat spray **(Conductor)**
Various shop signs, including "LAUNDERETTE" **(Actors)**
Washing machine with dial **(Actors)**
Basket of washing **(Customer)**
Net **(Mumps, Larry)**
Juggling balls **(Barker)**
Fake "weights" **(Mr Mighty)**
Wrestling ring, stools **(Actors)**
Bell **(Barker/Referee)**
Bottle of medicine **(Keeper)**

LIGHTING PLOT

Property fittings required: nil
A bare stage
To open: Overall general lighting

Light cues may be inserted at the discretion of the producer, or the lighting can remain constant throughout

EFFECTS PLOT

Cue 1	**Tickle** takes stock *Music or sounds*	(Page 3)
Cue 2	**Proprietor** exits *Vacuum cleaner noises*	(Page 6)
Cue 3	**Tickle:** "All right, I'll ask." *Traffic noises—climaxing in chaos*	(Page 7)
Cue 4	**Street-Cleaner** is about to throw paper in bin *Siren or alarm clock goes off*	(Page 12)
Cue 5	**Street-Cleaner** writhes on floor *Ambulance siren sounds—repeat as ambulance leaves*	(Page 12)
Cue 6	**Attendant:** "There she goes." *Washing machine noises*	(Page 21)
Cue 7	**Barker** enters *Circus music*	(Page 24)

N.B. Most, if not all, of these sounds can be vocalised by the cast.

MADE AND PRINTED IN GREAT BRITAIN BY
LATIMER TREND & COMPANY LTD PLYMOUTH
MADE IN ENGLAND